# FOLLOW THAT STAR

By

## DEANA V. SIMPSON

**Follow That Star**

**Copyright © 2011 Deana V. Simpson**

**ISBN – 13:978-1470122904**

This book is dedicated to: The one who guides and shines brightly in the dark night, in our life's journey. Jesus, who will eternally shine and never grow dim or fade away; Jesus, our bright and morning star.  Also to my husband, companion star, partner, and love in life, Mike Simpson.

# CONTENTS

# Preface

I found reading about stars fascinating. I could see many beautiful things to be compared with our journey following Jesus. God speaks to us in many ways. We just need to take the time and Behold, look around and see the greatness of God.

We need to surrender to God and let the creator create. God wants to make us something beautiful and do beautiful work in our lives. We need a fusion to take place in us. Fusion is melting together by heat. When stars are created this happens, which is powerful; much energy is released. Our spirit needs to be one with God's spirit; through Jesus this is possible. Jesus prayed to the Father in John 17, that we may be one with them, as Jesus is one with the Father. The Holy Spirit will do the melting in our hearts and minds, if we allow him. This is our ultimate end, union and oneness with our Savior and God.

My desire is that when you behold the beauty of the heavens and stars, you will draw closer to God. When you see God's greatness you will give Him praise. May you always follow the bright morning star Jesus and be transformed and shine like the stars for His honor and glory. Amen.

**Jeremiah 32:17, Oh, Lord God! Behold, Thou has made the heavens and the earth by thy great power and stretched out arm. And there is nothing too hard for Thee!**

**Rosette Nebula**

# Chapter One

## Our Nature and Stars

We have a lot in common with stars. God created us both, beginning with dust to dust. The birth process of stars and humans is hidden at first. Stars are born in clouds made of gas and dust, like a type of womb. The ingredients within come together and nuclear fusion must occur for stars to emerge into existence. If a fusion doesn't occur, a brown dwarf will remain a want-to-be star. Humans' birth process takes place in the mother's womb before emerging into view.

Stars develop into maturity, grow old, and die. Stars eventually run out of fuel and most fade away. They go through phases and changes in their lifetimes. Main sequence stars change from red giants to white dwarfs. Humans also go through changes, grow old, and die.

Stars differ from one another in their color, mass, brightness, and size. We also are different in looks, personalities, and talents. "For one star differeth from another star in glory" (I Corinthians 15:41).

Stars were created to give light in the night. We should be like the stars, giving light in a dark world. Without Jesus we are in spiritual darkness. Jesus is the true light: "I am the light of the world: he that followeth me shall not walk in darkness, but shall have the light of life" (John 8:12). There is hope in Jesus. His light restores and brings life.

We need a fusion to take place in us like the stars, in order to shine. Let the daystar arise in your hearts (II Peter 1:19). Jesus is that star, the morning star. We need a second birth, the star Jesus in our hearts. In John 3:3 Jesus says, "Except a man be born again, he cannot see the kingdom of God." Nicodemus came to Jesus one dark night, looking for light and truth. He didn't understand Jesus' words; how can an old man go back into his mother's womb? Jesus said, "Except a man be born of water and of the Spirit, he cannot enter into the kingdom of God" (John 3:5). This starts our journey to a new, spiritual awakening and life. Jesus is the Way, the Truth, and the Life.

The three wise men took a journey and it was a star they followed, that led them to Jesus to worship him. We should be wise, follow Jesus, and worship him. Then be a star for his glory, to lead others to him. "And they that be wise shall shine as the brightness, of the firmament; and they that turn many to righteousness as the stars for ever and ever" (Daniel 12:3). When we experience this spiritual birth we carry his light and shall be transformed into his likeness. "Ye are the light of the world; let your light so shine..." (Matthew 5:14, 16). "Who shall change our vile body, that it may be fashioned like unto his glorious body" (Philippians 3:21). In Matthew 17:2, Jesus was transfigured before his disciples and his face did shine as the sun, and his raiment was white as the light. This change starts inside you then outwardly.

We share a very interesting element with the stars. All the atoms that make up our solar system were forged in the furnace of the sun. Which means; that the atoms in our bodies were once part of a star. There is a twinkle in our eyes; we have star potential. Life is a gift from God. We need to allow the Creator of light to develop and grow in our being. Be a star for Jesus. "Every good gift and every perfect gift is from above, and cometh down from the Father of lights, with whom is no variableness, neither shadow of turning" (James 1:17). Jesus is the perfect gift from God to us.

In order for stars to continue to shine on, they must burn. Hydrogen must get converted into helium; we need a conversion to take place in us also. Four atoms of hydrogen get crushed in order to make one atom of helium. This can be compared to the daily process of putting off the old nature, and putting on Christ's divine nature.

We need to be burning and shining lights. Jesus spoke of John the Baptist as a burning and shining light in John 5:35. We must keep our light burning. The fuel we need is the oil, the anointing of the Holy Spirit within us. We are the lamps that need oil (Matthew 25:1-13). We can experience Jesus, and have a burning heart. The two disciples on the way to the village of Emmaus met Jesus, and their hearts burned within them (Luke 24:32).

# Chapter Two

## The Sun and Savior

The sun is a star, which is the source of life. Can you imagine what the world would be like without the sun? We couldn't exist, no light, growth, warmth, energy, sunrises, or sunsets. It would be a catastrophe. Everything would be affected. The sun is the light of our lives and we depend on it.

Jesus is our bright and morning star (Revelation 22:16). The Lord God is a sun and shield (Psalm 84:11). Now imagine if we didn't have the Savior Jesus. We couldn't exist: no hope, light, life, love, healing, and salvation "nothing." We would be doomed to death and hell. Isaiah 9:2 tells of the coming of Christ, the people that dwell in the land of the shadow of death, upon them hath the light shined; "There shall come a Star out of Jacob, and a Scepter shall rise out of Israel" (Numbers 24:17). Jesus' light is greater than the sun and should be the light of our lives. Each day we should depend on him and trust him.

In our solar system, the sun is the center and eight major planets revolve around it in closed orbits. The sun is a huge, self-luminous body and earth like the size of a pea. In the past men believed that the earth was at the center and everything revolved around us. The truth was discovered, but not accepted; it took time. Copernicus and Galileo were lights of truth in a dark age. It can be humbling to find out everything doesn't revolve around us. In our lives, once Christ is in us, a change should begin, from being self-centered to Christ-centered. Our aim should be to revolve around Christ and his teachings. Not our will but his will be done.

God created everything and we didn't come into existence on our own. "And God said, Let there be light: and there was light" (Genesis 1:3). God's gift to us the true light, his Son Jesus. "For God, who commanded the light to shine out of darkness, hath shined in our hearts, to give the light of the knowledge of the glory of God in the face of Jesus Christ" (II Corinthians 4:6).

There is something beautiful that takes place with the sun, a total solar eclipse. It is one of nature's most spectacular events. The moon passes directly between the sun and the earth, casting a shadow on the surface of the earth. It looks as if the moon has blocked out the light of the sun. One observable phenomenon, the sun's corona, a region of the sun's atmosphere, becomes visible. Normally, it is invisible because its light is completely lost in the brightness of the sun. The corona, when seen, is unforgettable.

There are two events I want to compare the solar eclipse to. The first is a total eclipse of the heart. When you are born of the spirit and turn to God in repentance, the Holy Spirit overshadows your heart, and for a moment you see the dark things in your heart. You realize they shouldn't be there and you need this experience. You accept it, to receive the gift of salvation, forgiveness, light, and healing. Then all of a sudden the Lord's light shines forth in your heart like a spectacular corona. The dark things go away and you are full of light. When things seem the darkest, the light can shine the brightest. "Arise, shine; for thy light is come, and the glory of the Lord is risen upon thee" (Isaiah 60:1). "A new heart also will I give you, and a new spirit, will I put within you…" (Ezekiel 36:26). "But unto you that fear my name shall the Sun of righteousness arise with healing in his wings…" (Malachi 4:2).

Jesus' death and resurrection is the second event. When Christ died all hope seemed lost. It didn't look like a victory was won. There was darkness over all the earth; the sun was darkened (Luke 23:44, 45). Jesus carried the sins of the world on the cross. Jesus died for us and rose again. Then his light shined in the land of the shadow of death, like a corona, and set the captives free. In I Peter 3:18-20, Jesus preached to the spirits of the Old Testament from prison in Hades. How exciting this whole event must have been; this truly was unforgettable. Not only did Christ rise from the dead, but the saints who slept arose. The saints came out of the graves after his resurrection and went into the holy city, and appeared unto many (Matthew 27:52, 53). Christ made many appearances. Jesus truly is the resurrection and the life. "He that believeth in me, though he were dead, yet shall he live: And whosoever liveth and believeth in me shall never die. Believest thou this?" (John 11:25, 26). Jesus conquered sin and death. How we can thank God for all this, we who are victorious through Jesus Christ our Lord! "Jesus Christ, who abolished death, and hath brought life and immortality to light through the gospel" (II Timothy 1:10). Jesus through death destroyed him that had the power of death that is the devil (Hebrews 2:14-15).

# Chapter Three

## Our Decisions

Once we make the decision to follow Jesus, we will continue to have to make many more decisions in our lives. What is our destiny? Where do we belong? The choice is ours to make. As we seek guidance from our morning star Jesus, his plan will unfold. Even when trials come in our lives we can allow them to produce something beautiful like a nebula or we can allow them to destroy us and turn us into a black hole. The choice is ours: heaven or hell. Jesus wants to make us something beautiful for his glory. Each of us is unique in our own way with special gifts and talents.

When a star is very massive and dying, unless it sheds or loses a large amount of its mass, the star will be unable to resist gravity and the core will collapse, blowing the star apart. A spectacular, supernova explosion takes place. The surviving remains can turn into a nebula. Nebulae contain gas and dust from which new stars are born. A nebula or cloud will not shine without a brilliant hot star. Some of the nebulae have become the birth place of stars.

The Orion Nebula, a star nursery, has several hot young stars embedded within. The Horsehead is a dark nebula. The most famous, the Crab Nebula, is all that is left of a mighty explosion witnessed by many in 1054. The Eagle Nebula is a combination of nebula and star clusters. A few other nebulae are the Clownface Nebula and Ring Nebula. There are many more nebulae and each is unique in its own way.

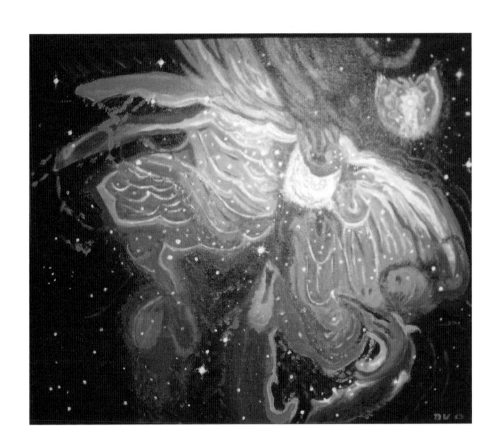

**Orion Nebula**

Sometimes in our lives, everything falls apart. It could be a health failure, a job loss or a death in the family. It just happens, an explosion in our lives and we have no control of it. As we turn to God in our brokenness something good can come of it. God's grace is great. As we shed our ways and surrender to God, something new can give birth in us. It could be healing, a new job, new relationships, or new experiences.

The apostle Paul said in the Bible, "I die daily," that is, to himself. God told him his grace was sufficient. Some encouraging scriptures: "For I reckon that the sufferings of this present time are not worthy to be compared with the glory which shall be revealed in us." "And we know that all things work together for good to them that love God" (Romans 8:18, 28). "Blessed is the man that endureth temptation: for when he is tried, he shall receive the crown of life, which the Lord hath promised to them that love him" (James 1:12). "Behold, the former things are come to pass, and new things do I declare..." (Isaiah 42:9). God can turn your life into a beautiful nebula.

When I think of Christ and his disciples, the way they lived and died, they truly brought an explosion of light, hope, and change. They impacted the world like never before. They left a remnant that still exists today. The deaths of the martyrs of the early church didn't end the church, but gave birth to many more believers and followers of Christ. The church is alive because Jesus is alive.

When a supernova explosion takes place, it is the gas blown off from the star sweeping up other gas from the interstellar medium that forms a supernova remnant.

**Supernova Star Explosion**

After the explosion all that remains of the collapsed core is known as a neutron or pulsar star. Neutron stars are very small but can spin many times in a second. These stars give out a flash of energy, like a lighthouse. There is, however, another fate that can take place in a massive star: it can become a black hole. The matter of the neutron star gets squeezed so tightly that the weight becomes unbearable for it. The strength of gravity shrinks it until it disappears. The star gets crushed out of existence, turning into a black hole. It is so important that we lay our burdens down at the cross. Hebrews 12:1 tells us to lay aside every weight and sin, which easily besets us. Apart from Christ we can do nothing. The blood of Jesus cleanses us from all sin (I John 1:7).

Nothing can escape a black hole once inside, not even light. A black hole can be compared to hell: though unseen, it exists and the dragon the devil devours people in it. Once someone is pulled in there is no escape; it's too late. "Be sober, be vigilant; because your adversary the devil, as a roaring lion, walketh about, seeking whom he may devour" (I Peter 5:8). The devil wants to take as many people as he can with him. "Therefore hell hath enlarged herself, and opened her mouth, without measure..." (Isaiah 5:14). Hell is a place of darkness and torment. "And this is the condemnation, that light is come into the world, and man loved darkness rather than light, because their deeds were evil" (John 3:19).

Satan once was a bright star but fell and was cast down. "How art thou fallen from heaven, O Lucifer, son of the morning! How art thou cut down to the ground, which didst weaken the nations!" (Isaiah 14:12). We must continue in the faith, and not let our hearts harden or let Satan fill our hearts with his lies and darkness. "But he that endureth to the end shall be saved" (Matthew 10:22). "The night is far spent, the day is at hand: let us therefore cast off the works of darkness, and let us put on the armour of light." "The light of the body is the eye: if therefore thine eye be single, thy whole body shall be full of light" (Matthew 6:22). Our eyes should be single on Jesus.

More than half the stars have at least one companion star. There are many different types of stars, double, binary or multiple, variables, Cepheid variables, and star clusters. In our lives we need to find our place and calling, like the stars. There are different colors, blue being the hottest, white, yellow, orange, and red being the coolest. How on fire are we for Jesus? Even the smallest star is a huge ball of burning gas that gives off enormous amounts of light and heat. God can use you. "Who maketh his angels spirits, and his ministers a flame of fire" (Hebrews 1:7).

Some stars can change in brightness. Some that have a dramatic change can change in size and color also. Those with a slight change in this existence are called variable stars. One type, the Cepheid, grows cooling and dimming, then shrinks and heats up, getting brighter again, starting the cycle over. We, like the Cepheid variable, need change in our lives; it's up to us if it is slight or dramatic. How much of Christ do you want in you, to shine forth? "He must increase, but I must decrease," said John the Baptist (John 3:30). We are to grow in grace, but know there is a battle going on between our flesh and the spirit, and they are contrary to each other. The works of the flesh bring death, not the kingdom of God. The spirit brings life and we must walk and be led by the spirit. When we let the flesh grow we become cooler toward God; we grow dimmer. The spirit wins when we crucify the flesh with its affections and lusts we shrink; the spirit heats up and the Holy Spirit shines brighter again, like the Cepheid variable.

The choice is ours but we are to press toward the mark for the prize of the high calling of God in Christ Jesus. Reach out for the morning star in Revelation 2:28.

There are large groups of stars so close together and gravitationally bound together that form a globelike structure, called globular clusters. The Great Globular Cluster seen through a telescope looks like a mass of thousands of stars. I think of this cluster as the church, bound together by the Holy Spirit. "For as the body is one, and hath many members, and all the members of that one body, being many are one body: so also is Christ. For by one Spirit are we all baptized into one body, whether we be Jews or Gentiles, whether we be bond or free; and have been all made to drink into one Spirit. The body is not one member, but has many members" (I Corinthians 12:12-14).

There is another type of cluster, an open, loose group of stars also held together by gravity. The Pleiades or seven sisters is an example, seven stars that can be seen with the naked eye, but consisting of hundreds of stars, 50 million years old. I think of Revelation, when John saw seven candlesticks and in Jesus' right hand seven stars. The seven stars are seven angel-messengers of the seven churches, which are the seven candlesticks. Seven is a very significant number in the Bible, representing both the seven churches and seven phases of the spiritual history of the church, from 96 A.D. to the end.

There are binary stars, two stars connected, that revolve around each other. Multiple stars are more than two stars forming together and orbiting one another. I think of the scripture, "For where two or three are gathered together in my name, there am I in the midst of them"

## The Pleiades Star Cluster

(Matthew 18:20). Jesus had an inner circle, Peter, James, and John. We need an inner circle in our walk also.

There are double stars that look like one star but with a telescope you can see two. This reminds me of marriage: "Wherefore they are no more twain, but one flesh" (Matthew 19:5, 6). There are some beautiful double stars, such as the Albireo (B Cygni). The primary star is yellow-orange with a magnitude brightness of 3 and the second star is bluish with a magnitude brightness of 5. We can complement one other with our uniqueness.

## Chapter Four

## A Heavenly View

Even though our view of the universe has improved, we are still limited in seeing beyond our Local Group. The Local Group consists of about thirty galaxies, including the Andromeda Galaxy M31, the largest member, and our own Milky Way, the second-largest member. Our galaxy group is a cluster; along with other such clusters we are part of a Local Super-cluster. It is estimated there are millions of super-clusters in the universe. We can begin to see how great the heavens and universe are. Yet in I Kings 8:27 it says, "Behold, the heaven and heaven of heavens cannot contain thee." How great is God! In the Bible Job declares that God alone spreads out the heavens and made Arcturus, Orion, and Pleiades (Job 9:8, 9).

Part of man's problem is we view things with earthly eyes in an earthly realm. We need to see things as Jesus does from His heavenly view. "Seek those things which are above, where Christ sitteth on the right hand of God" (Colossians 3:1). In Christ, this view can be ours now, "And hath raised us up together, and made us sit together in heavenly places in Christ Jesus" (Ephesians 2:6).

Our universe is expanding and changing more and more. The matter that is visible, the stars, dust, and gas, is only a small part in the universe. Two other ingredients are invisible, dark matter and dark energy believed to comprise 95 percent of the universe. It's interesting that more of the unseen exists than the seen.

It shouldn't be hard to believe that the spiritual realms and heavens exist. God spoke to Job and said, where were you when I laid the foundations? In Job 38:4, 33 God asks Job more questions, "Knowest thou the ordinances of heaven?" Man has sought truth about the universe, how much more should we seek the truth and mysteries of God's heavenly kingdom? "But seek ye first the kingdom of God, and his righteousness" (Matthew 6:33).

The apostle Paul in II Corinthians 12:2 says, "I knew a man in Christ above fourteen years ago (whether in the body, I cannot tell: or whether out of the body, I cannot tell: God knoweth), such an one caught up to the third heaven." This was a very real experience and is proof of the existence of a spiritual realm.

We need to have a new spiritual perspective, which believes. The words of Jesus to Thomas in John 20:29: "Jesus saith unto him, Thomas, because thou hast seen me, thou hast believed: blessed are they that have not seen, and yet have believed."

We can have experiences in the spirit as we follow Jesus. The Holy Spirit will lead and guide us into all truth. "Howbeit when he, the Spirit of truth, is come he will guide you into all truth..." (John 16:13). By the power of the Holy Spirit we can have a personal relationship with Jesus Christ.

# Chapter Five

## Our Hope

"Seek him that maketh the seven stars and Orion, and turneth the shadow of death into the morning, and maketh the day dark with night" (Amos 5:8). We should be looking up for the return of Jesus. Jesus is hidden from our view he is up in heaven, sitting at the Father's right hand making intercession for us. Way above the clouds, stars, and galaxies, too far away from our natural eyes to behold. We need to have the eyes of the spirit and be expectant. For Jesus shall return in the clouds for us, his bride. This is our blessed hope; Jesus is our only hope.

There is something very special about clouds, in the sky, stars, and galaxies but most of all in the Bible. Things happen in clouds not just in the natural but in the spiritual realm. It is very exciting but the most exciting is yet to come: Jesus' return in a cloud for us.

Jesus was taken up, and a cloud received him in Acts 1:9-11. The disciples looked steadfastly, toward heaven as he went up; behold, two men stood by them in white apparel and said, "Ye men of Galilee, why stand ye gazing up into heaven? This same Jesus, which is taken up from you into heaven, shall so come in like manner as ye have seen him go into heaven."

Our Milky Way Galaxy is only one; there are close to one hundred billion galaxies in the universe. No two galaxies are exactly alike. Each has its own unique appearance.

**Spiral Galaxy**

Our galaxy is active, a barred spiral with about 200 billion stars, large numbers of nebulae, star clusters, and uncounted planets. It is an enormous star island, with dense clouds of stars and lanes of dust. We have a cloudy band of light made of billions of stars. This cloudy band is glorious; how much more glorious is heaven, where God the Most High sits.

Another reason clouds are special: God manifested his presence to Moses and the children of Israel in a pillar of a cloud. When the Israelites left Egypt, God led them in a cloud by day and a pillar of fire by night. When the cloud moved they followed. God also showed his power and glory in a cloud in Exodus 40:34-38, when a cloud covered the tent of the congregation, and the shekinah glory of the Lord filled the tabernacle. Moses wasn't even able to enter the tent, because the cloud abode there.

In II Chronicles 5:13, 14, Solomon built the temple, a home for the ark, of the covenant. At the dedication of the temple, as they were praising and thanking the Lord, the temple was filled with a cloud. "So that the priests could not stand to minister by reason of the cloud: for the glory of the Lord had filled the house of God."

When Jesus was transfigured, his face shone like the sun, his clothing became dazzling white, and while he yet spoke, a bright cloud overshadowed them and a voice out of the cloud, said, "This is my beloved Son, in whom I am well pleased; hear ye him" (Matthew 17:5).

The light that shines forth from the cloud is bright and beautiful. Stars are born in the clouds. We need the cloud of God to overshadow us, and the Holy Spirit to fill us, like the

# Jesus In The Clouds

glory of God filled the temple, to experience rebirth, so we can be a star for the Lord. Now our bodies are the temples of the Holy Spirit.

It is no wonder that our morning star Jesus shall return in a cloud. "Behold, the Lord rideth upon a swift cloud…" (Isaiah 19:1). There is a great history of the cloud of God. There is more to come, "and then shall they see the Son of man coming in a cloud with power and great glory" (Luke 21:27).

Our hope is receiving our new body, a spiritual body, a heavenly body like our risen Savior. Christ in us is the hope of glory. "Beloved, now are we the sons of God, and it doth not yet appear what we shall be: but we know that, when he shall appear, we shall be like him; for we shall see him as he is" (I John 3:2).

Our blessed hope is to fly as a cloud to be raptured. "Then we which are alive and remain shall be caught up together with them in the clouds, to meet the Lord in the air: and so shall we ever be with the Lord" (I Thessalonians 4:16, 18). "In a moment, in the twinkling of an eye, at the last trump..." (I Corinthians 15:51-53), we shall be changed; we shall receive an incorruptible body.

We are warned to watch and pray, that we may be accounted worthy to escape that great tribulation that shall befall the world. People need to make the decision to follow the Lord. Behold, He comes quickly and there will be a day of darkness coming.

Be ready, he comes with clouds, and every eye shall see him, and they also, which pierced him: and all kindreds of the earth shall wail because of him. Even Enoch, from the Old

Testament, prophesied saying, "Behold, the Lord cometh with ten thousands of his saints" (Jude verse 14).

The kingdoms of this world shall become the kingdoms of our Lord, and of Christ. The bride of Christ shall reign with him for a thousand years. "And saviours shall come up on mount Zion to judge the mount of Esau, and the kingdom shall be the Lord's" (Obadiah verse 21).

# Chapter Six

## Our Marriage

"And I John saw the holy city, new Jerusalem, coming down from God out of heaven, prepared as a bride adorned for her husband" (Revelation 21:2). The Church of Christ is the future bride of the Lamb Jesus. We have a beautiful wedding and marriage to look forward to. Our marriage will have the greatest love of all. Just as a bride makes herself ready for her wedding day so should the Church. In Revelation 19:7 it says "the marriage of the Lamb is come, and his wife hath made herself ready." Our Bridegroom Jesus has made preparations for us, for that joyful, special time and celebration. John 14 is a beautiful passage and love story. The Lord tells us not to be troubled as in His Father's house are many mansions, and He goes to prepare a place for us. Jesus says, "I will come again and receive you unto myself: that where I am, there ye may be also."

Meanwhile on earth the picture won't be so pretty. Already you can see things getting worse in the world. Violence, wars, and terrorist attacks. Even in the galaxies there is violence, cannibalism, and collisions. Bigger galaxies eat smaller galaxies. In the Antennae two galaxies collided, NGC 4038 and NGC 4039. In NGC 7252 a merger took place and it survived. During these violent clashes star clusters were created. You can imagine how crowded it got.

Just as a star collapses and can turn into a black hole, so can globular clusters. Some very interesting things that happen for survival are: stars begin to interact with one other forming a binary system, holding them together. Stars pair up and some merge. Two smaller stars merge into one, becoming a blue straggler, which is bluer and brighter than main sequence stars.

**Whirlpool Interacting Galaxies**

You can find these blue stragglers in NGC 6397 and 47Tucanae clusters. What a beautiful example of coming together during a crisis. We can learn something from the stars. Stars need one another and we need one another.

It is the love of God that will keep His church, His bride together. God's love will see us through. It is important that we love God with all our hearts and love one another. Psalm 145:20 says, "The Lord preserveth all them that love him: but all the wicked will he destroy." "A new commandment I give unto you, that ye love one another" (John 13:34). Love never fails and though there is faith, hope, and love, the greatest is love. Love will abide forever (I Corinthians 13).

Jesus showed us His love already on the cross, bearing our sins and punishment. "Greater love hath no man than this, that a man lay down his life for his friends" (John 15:13). The words of the song, "Oh, How He Loves You and Me"..."He gave His life, what more could He give" what a love we have in Jesus and what a wonderful marriage we will have, a heavenly, everlasting one that will be forever.

## Chapter Seven

## Our Outcome

"And they overcame him by the blood of the Lamb, and by the word of their testimony" (Revelation 12:11). "He that hath the Son hath life; and he that hath not the Son of God hath not life" (I John 5:12). The outcome of the believer is eternal life and an expected end. The overcomers shall have a bright and beautiful ending. "Then shall the righteous shine forth as the sun in the kingdom of their Father" (Matthew 13:43). Our final destination, the Holy City, New Jerusalem, will have no need of the sun, neither of the moon, to shine in it; the glory of God will lighten it, and the Lamb shall be the light thereof.

What will become of our planet, sun, and universe? The universe is expanding; will it continue to expand forever or will it stop and shrink? Our sun is middle-aged; there is about another 5 or 6 billion years before it becomes a red giant. How will man survive in the far future of the universe?

The creation of the universe was a smooth beginning. The creator God, the great master designer, knew what he was doing. God said the word and it was. Everything was done in order. God is not only the master designer but master planner as well. God has a plan for us and the Bible tells of our beginnings in Genesis and our endings in Revelation. The contact we each need to make is with God, through his Son Jesus. We can receive the truth only with an open heart; our minds will only get in the way. Some things can't be explained with our intellect; we need to just believe. The just shall live by faith.

When you look at our Milky Way Galaxy, other galaxies, and our solar system, you can see the greatness of God. Our planet Earth alone, how perfect it is for life, called the Goldilocks planet. The earth is just right for us and it is unique. There may be other stars with planets but not like ours. Each star, planet, and galaxy is different. "The heavens declare the glory of God; and the firmament sheweth his handy work" (Psalm 19:1). "Lift up your eyes on high, and behold who hath created these things, that bringeth out their host by number: he calleth them all by names by the greatness of his might, for that he is strong in power; not one faileth" (Isaiah 40:26).

As beautiful as the heavens and earth seem, they are polluted by sin. "The stars are not pure in his sight" (Job 25:5). The fall of Lucifer brought sin in the universe. The fall of man (fallen Adam) brought the curse of sin and death. Corruption entered the earth, and violence. Satan polluted heaven, where the stars are; the pollution of sin contaminated the earth, animals, and people. Everything was affected and suffered. "For we know that the whole creation groaneth and travaileth in pain together until now" (Romans 8:22).

Black holes are destructive, regions of no return. The super massive black holes devour galaxies. It was discovered in 1998 that there is a super massive black hole in the center of our Milky Way Galaxy. It is in the process of consuming its smaller neighbors, two nearby irregular galaxies, the Large and Small Magellanic Clouds. It is estimated that within another ten billion years, the Milky Way will have swallowed all the matter in the clouds and the two neighboring galaxies will no longer exist.

The good news is God has a master plan. After the one-thousand-year reign with Christ, the devil and his followers will be cast into the lake of fire; God shall make all things new. As we have been transformed, the creation will be transformed into a beautiful New Paradise. It shall be renewed and purged from the pollution of sin. There will be total restoration. "And I saw a new heaven and a new earth: for the first heaven and the first earth were passed away" (Revelation 21:1, 2).

Heaven will not be limited by time and space. It will be possible to explore an unlimited universe. Our new home, the Holy, New Jerusalem, shall descend out of heaven from God. God shall dwell with us and be our God. God shall wipe away all tears: there will be no more death, sorrow, crying, or pain: for the former things will have passed away. We shall reign with Christ forever. This is our expected end.

The story of Joseph had a beautiful and expected end. In Genesis 37:9, Joseph dreamed a dream more; and behold, the sun and the moon and the eleven stars made obeisance to him. The meaning; his mother, father, and eleven brothers would someday bow down to him. God would raise Joseph up. Joseph would go through much sorrow, pain, and trials first. The dream came true: eventually Pharaoh made Joseph ruler over all the land in Egypt. In Genesis 41:40-44, Joseph was given the Pharaoh's ring, and was arrayed in fine linen, and received a gold chain on his neck. Joseph was given authority to rule Egypt.

This story can be compared to the blessings of our new life in the kingdom of God. We shall reign with Christ as priests and kings. We shall be rewarded for our faithfulness. We too, should hang onto the vision or dream the Lord has given us. In the midst of life's trials we have hope. The Lord said in Jeremiah 29:11, "For I know the thoughts that I think toward you, saith the Lord, thoughts of peace, and not of evil, to give you an expected end."

**The Nativity**

# Conclusion

It was reported by Chinese astronomers that in 5 B.C., in March a "guest star" appeared over Bethlehem at the time of Jesus' birth.

This was a special star, as everything about Jesus coming into this world was special. A virgin gave birth to Jesus as recorded in Matthew 1:20-23, angels appeared unto shepherds (Luke 2:8-14), and the three wise men from the east saw His star and came to worship Him, bearing gifts (Matthew 2:1-11).

If you would like to know this special star Jesus personally, just pray:

Dear Lord Jesus,

I know I am a sinner and need your forgiveness. I believe you died on the cross for my sins and rose again. Forgive me of all my sins, and come into my heart and life. Be my Lord, and Savior, make me a new creature for your glory.

In Jesus' name,

Amen.

**Luke 2:14, Glory to God in the highest, and on earth peace, good will toward men.**

God made beautiful promises to Abraham in Genesis. We can now obtain these promises through Jesus Christ. Genesis 15:5-6 says, "Look now toward heaven, and tell the stars, if thou be able to number them: and he said unto him, so shall thy seed be." In Galatians 3:16, it says that Christ is that seed. We are the descendents through Jesus and are compared to the stars in heaven. What a wonderful tribute.

Abraham believed in the Lord and it was counted to him for righteousness. Abraham was a hundred years old and Sarah ninety years when Isaac was born. We need to believe in God's promises and wait on God. As Genesis 18:14 says, "Is anything too hard for the Lord? At the time appointed I will return unto thee." Maranatha--Our Lord Cometh!

## Resources

David H. Levy, Skywatching (U.S. Welden Owen Inc., 1994).

John Gribbin, Hyperspace (DK Publishing Inc., 2001, our final frontier).

Discovery Channel: Night Sky-An Explore Your World Handbook (Discovery Books, 1999).

The First Scofield Reference Bible, Containing Old and New Testaments, Authorized King James Version (Barbour and Co. Inc., 1986).

Astronomy Magazine Explore and discover (Kalmbach Publishing Co., Nov. issue 2003).